Niagara Falls

An 1890 photograph of Niagara Falls with Goat Island in the foreground.

Niagara Falls

by Robert West Howard

illustrated with photographs

Franklin Watts, Inc.
575 Lexington Avenue
New York, N.Y. 10022

For Scott Barrett Howard

Photographs courtesy of:

Buffalo & Erie Historical Society: page 65
National Film Board of Canada: page 70
New York Historical Society: pages 12, 59, 61
New York State Library: pages 20, 35, 44, 49, 52
Old Fort Niagara Assn. (by Grove McClellan): page 14
Ontario Archives: pages 36, 40
Ontario Dept. of Tourism and Information: page 17
Ontario Hydro: pages 6, 75, 76
Power Authority of the State of New York: page 78
Public Archives of Canada: opp. title page, pages 5, 9, 19, 22, 24, 25, 28, 30, 31, 38, 47,
    53, 56, 63, 68, 69, 73

Cover photo courtesy Public Archives of Canada

Contents

The Great Throatway   3

The Canoemen   8

Three Flags   15

Land of Promise   27

Dread Frontier   34

The Canawlers   46

Honeymooners' Paradise   51

The Daredevils   58

Becoming Good Neighbors   67

Niagara Power   72

A Niagara Chronology   80

Index   87

Niagara Falls

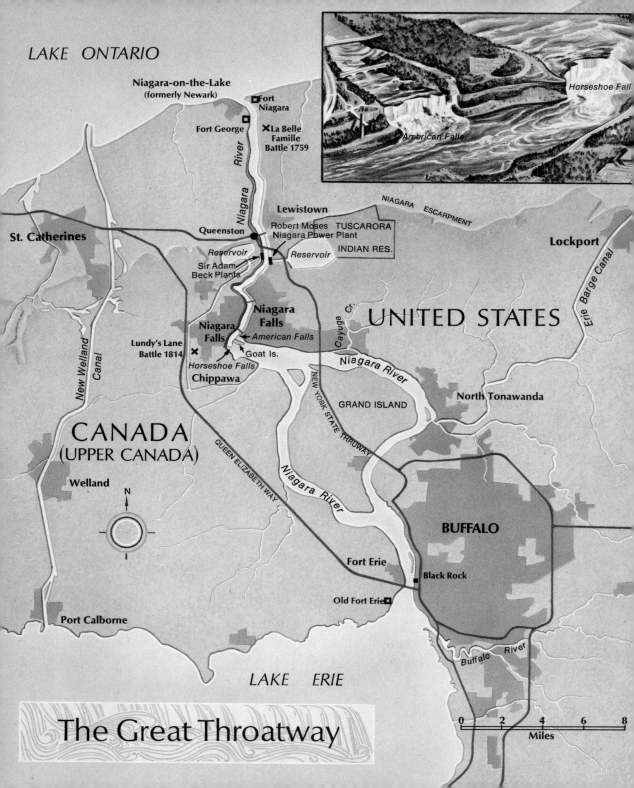

LAKE ONTARIO

Niagara-on-the-Lake
(formerly Newark)

Fort Niagara

Fort George

×La Belle Famille Battle 1759

River

Niagara

St. Catherines

Lewistown

Queenston

Robert Moses Niagara Power Plant

TUSCARORA

NIAGARA ESCARPMENT

Lockport

Reservoir

Sir Adam Beck Plants

Reservoir

INDIAN RES.

Erie Barge Canal

Niagara Falls

New Welland Canal

Niagara Falls

American Falls

Cayuga Cr.

UNITED STATES

Lundy's Lane Battle 1814

×

Goat Is.

Horseshoe Falls

Niagara River

Chippawa

North Tonawanda

New York State Thruway

GRAND ISLAND

CANADA
(UPPER CANADA)

Niagara River

Welland

N

Queen Elizabeth Way

BUFFALO

Fort Erie

Port Calborne

Old Fort Erie

Black Rock

LAKE ERIE

Buffalo River

American Falls

Horseshoe Fall

0   2   4   6   8
Miles

The Great Throatway

The Great Throatway

Niagara Falls is the most famous and most important waterfall on earth. Between 1640 and 1900, Indian massacres, savage battles, refugee slaves, canalboats, daredevils, and honeymooners brought Niagara Falls its fame. Its importance has been established by the gigantic Niagara power plants developed there since 1881 and the locks of the St. Lawrence Seaway that enable ocean ships to climb around the falls.

Niagara Falls is, the longest, steepest step in the Niagara River's 36-mile-long drop from its headwaters on Lake Erie — 570 feet above sea level — to its mouth on Lake Ontario — 244 feet above sea level. Four of the five Great Lakes feed water into the Niagara's channel. The flow of water into the Niagara averages 202,000 cubic feet — about 1,500,000 gallons — per second. Only two of the thousands of waterfalls on earth are larger than Niagara Falls.

The Seneca Indians gave the river and its falls the name *Niagara*. The word means "the great throat." It was a wise choice for a name. The Niagara is "the great throatway" of the inland sea that shimmers 2,000 miles from Minnesota, Illinois, and Wisconsin to Labrador and the Gaspé Peninsula at the mouth of the St. Lawrence River.

(3)

That was why Indian tribes battled to control its portage trail for many centuries and why France, Great Britain, and the United States struggled just as savagely there during the French and Indian Wars, the American Revolution, and the War of 1812. And, of course, that it also why the Niagara Power and Ontario Hydro generating plants in the Niagara Gorge today can produce 25.7 billion kilowatt hours of electrical energy each year for the homes and industries of 50 million Americans and 12 million Canadians.

Immense glaciers that formed on the northern half of North America millions of years ago carved out Niagara Falls. The weather was so cold for hundreds of centuries that the glacier ice cliffs grew as high as the tallest mountains in the Rockies are today. Then, for reasons that nobody understands, our climate changed. The ice cliffs began to melt.

This melt-off sent torrents of water and icebergs roaring across the northeastern third of North America. The flood plowed eastward toward the Atlantic Ocean. In time, it created two channels. One veered southeastward across central New York and down the Mohawk and Hudson valleys. The other gouged northeastward to create the valley of the St. Lawrence River.

By 20,000 B.C., these glacial floods had created the basins of the Great Lakes. But a ridge of hard rock encircled the southern and eastern shores of the four western lakes: Superior, Michigan, Huron, and Erie. The ridge served as a dam that held the water in Lake Erie 326 feet above the water in Lake Ontario.

This natural dam between Lakes Erie and Ontario is composed of several different kinds of rock. A tough, black rock

This massive dolomite boulder was named the "Rock of Ages" by guides who led tourists over the slippery catwalks to the Cave of the Winds. When LaSalle first viewed the Falls in the 1600's, the boulder was part of the floor of the Upper Rapids, above the Falls.

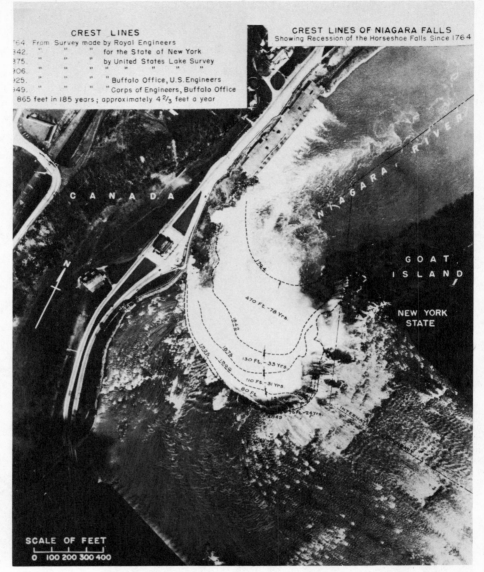

CREST LINES OF NIAGARA FALLS
Showing Recession of the Horseshoe Falls Since 1764

CREST LINES
'64. From Survey made by Royal Engineers
'42.   "   "   "   " for the State of New York
'75.   "   "   "   " by United States Lake Survey
'06.   "   "   "   "   " Buffalo Office, U.S. Engineers
'25.   "   "   "   "   " Buffalo Office, U.S. Engineers
'49.   "   "   "   "   " Corps of Engineers, Buffalo Office
865 feet in 185 years; approximately 4 2/3 feet a year

SCALE OF FEET
0 100 200 300 400

The steady retreat of Niagara Falls southward toward Lake Erie is shown by the dotted lines across this airplane photo of the Horseshoe Falls on Canada's side of the Niagara River. Between 1764, when engineers began recording the crest line, and 1850 the rushing Great Lakes water crumbled away almost six feet of rock each year. As the water levels of the lakes dropped, the grinding power decreased. Now the Falls are retreating southward at an average rate of two feet each year.

called *dolomite* is close to the surface. The dolomite lies atop a layer of softer, flaky rock called *shale*.

The flow-off waters gouged a path due south-to-north across the thirty-six miles of dolomite-on-shale from Lake Erie to Lake Ontario. Geologists believe that this flow-off first began to tumble over cliffs near what is now Lewiston. That was the first site of Niagara Falls.

The force of the water and the cracks created by freezing winter temperatures caused the soft shale under the dolomite to crumble. Then big chunks of the dolomite tumbled into the water, too.

As the rock wore away, the water flow of Niagara Falls began to move south towards Lake Erie. A deep rock-strewn gorge was left in its wake.

By the time the ancestors of the Indians moved into the region, about 5000 B.C., the Niagara Gorge was several miles long and the Falls were almost a hundred feet high. In those days, the water and ice were gouging the Falls southward fifteen feet each year.

The Canoemen

The invention of the canoe made Niagara Falls and its gorge extremely important to the Indians. Historians still have not determined exactly when the canoe was invented, but it was probably thought up and experimented with by hunters and fishermen between 2000 and 1000 B.C. Its birchbark hull, hickory ribs, and paddle were so light that two men could carry the craft across the forested cliffs between Lake Ontario and Lake Erie. Thus the Great Lakes waterway between east and west first became useful to the red men.

Obsidian arrowheads, pearl-shell ornaments, and copper tools dug up at ancient Indian village sites near Niagara Falls have provided archeologists with many clues about the great distances traveled by prehistoric traders. The obsidian arrowheads could only have come from Wyoming or Montana. The pearl buttons were canoed in and portaged from the Mississippi and Alabama shores of the Gulf of Mexico. The copper was paddled down from northern Michigan. Thus the canoe first made Niagara Falls a very important barrier to the red man — and a place worth capturing and fortifying.

The Ohio-New York area has changed greatly since the first Indians arrived there about 5000 B.C. At that time the walls of

Mohawk, Seneca, and Onondaga warriors brought lacrosse sticks as well as war hatchets to the ceremonial greeting they gave Great Britain's Prince Arthur at Brantford in 1869.

the glacier still glimmered on the north horizon, across present-day Ontario and Quebec. The water from their melt-off still formed lakes and whirlpools and foaming rivers that covered most of Ohio and New York. The principal drainage channel into the Atlantic poured through the two big land-troughs that we now call the Mohawk and Hudson River valleys.

Mammoths, the hairy elephants that had inhabited the region for thousands of years, still fed on tall grasses and tree leaves

(9)

along the lakeshores. Beaver built hundreds of log dams and reed huts in the creeks. Black bear, bison, and deer roamed the pine, hickory, and oak forests of the Niagara Gorge. Each spring hundreds of thousands of salmon and sturgeon — some of them ten feet long — struggled up the rapids to breed and give birth to babies in deep, shadowed pools below Niagara Falls.

This wealth of wild game first attracted Indians to the Niagara region. There were no schools, of course. But learning to fish and hunt and transform the catch into food and clothing and tools was more rigorous than studying books or reciting in class. Boys learned to make fishhooks and spears and to chip the knife-sharp edges on arrowheads before they were six years old. Grand-mothers were strict teachers for the young girls learning to sew, cook, cure skins, dry fish, and garden.

Then the invention of the canoe changed the red man's way of life. The canoe made it possible to take fishing and hunting expeditions all along the Great Lakes and down to the ocean. These "long hunts" began the trade for chunks of copper from Michigan, pieces of wampum shell from the New York and New Jersey seashore, and glistening pearl shell from the upper valley of the Mississippi River. The speedy travel by canoe encouraged warfare, too.

The early red men did not have a system of writing. So there is no record of the battles that must have been fought for control of the Niagara during the centuries after the invention of the canoe. But the ruins of an ancient fort have been discovered on Second Mountain, between Lewiston and the present site of Niagara Falls. Bones and tools found there have been identified as belonging to the Moundbuilders, the powerful Indian nation that built the serpent mounds in Ohio. By carbon-dating these remains, archeologists concluded that this first-known Niagara fort and customs post was built about A.D. 100.

Because Niagara was so important on the Great Lakes canoe journey, the Indians believed that Niagara Falls was the home of a powerful spirit-god. The legend developed that human sacrifices were once offered to this spirit-god. Each spring, according to the legend, the chiefs chose a young woman to become "the bride of the spirit-god." She was dressed in clothing made of doeskin and beaver fur, then placed in a new canoe, and sent over the Falls.

About the time that Norsemen from Greenland and Iceland were exploring the coasts of Newfoundland and Nova Scotia, the Niagara was conquered by invaders from the west. These invaders were taller, stronger, and more brutal than the tribesmen who lived on the Niagara. They are believed to have been members of the Aztec race that conquered Mexico and built its pyramids and walled cities.

When Columbus reached the West Indies on October 12, 1492, the descendants of these conquerors were fighting among themselves. One large tribe became known as the *Hurons*. Their villages were in the St. Lawrence valley and along the north shore of Lake Ontario.

Five other groups conquered the territory between present-day Rochester and Schenectady, New York. These Five Nations, as they became known, were, in west to east order of residence, the Senecas, Cayugas, Onondagas, Oneidas, and Mohawks. Be-

(11)

This was the Niagara Falls scene the British-Colonial conquerors of the "throatway" saw in 1760. Captain Thomas Davies of the Royal Artillery made this painting during 1777-78 while he was stationed at Fort Niagara.

tween 1550 and 1600, they allied into a confederacy. They called themselves *The Real People*.

On July 30, 1609, Samuel de Champlain and a party of Huron allies battled with a party of Mohawks on the shore of Lake Champlain. That same summer, Henry Hudson sailed his ship, the *Half Moon,* up the river that was later named for him. Hudson claimed the area for Holland.

The French and the Dutch were enemies. Both the French in the St. Lawrence Valley and the Dutch in the Hudson Valley were eager to trade for the huge harvests of beaver pelts controlled by the Hurons and the Five Nations.

The French route to the west and the Dutch route to the west met at the Niagara Gorge, and two centuries of warfare over its ownership began.

The three flags that fly above Fort Niagara are saluted twice daily by uniformed guards. The "House of Peace," built in the 1720's, is at center rear.

Three Flags

The friendship between the government of New France in the St. Lawrence Valley and the Hurons persuaded the Five Nations to become allies of the Hudson Valley Dutch and the New England Puritans. Five Nations warriors aided the Puritans in their wars with Massachusetts Indians. The Dutch and the Puritans gave the Five Nations guns in exchange for beaver pelts, corn, herbs, dried fruits, and maple sugar.

About 1640, the Five Nations began to plunder and burn the Huron villages along Lake Ontario. They drove the Hurons west to the shores of the lake now called Huron. That was when the Senecas conquered the Niagara Gorge and gained control of the portage trail around the falls. This forced the French to use the long Ottawa River-North Bay-Georgian Bay detour for their fur trade with the western Indians.

The French began to refer to the Five Nations as "the Iroquois," a derogatory name that had been thought up by the Hurons. In the Huron tongue, *Iroquois* means "the vipers who strike without warning."

The British conquered the Hudson Valley in 1664 and named it "New York." They made alliances with the Five Nations and were always careful to use the phrase "the Five Nations," rather than "Iroquois," in their official papers and public speeches. In 1722, after the Tuscarora tribe fled to western New York from the Carolina mountains, the official title of the great red-man confederacy became "the Six Nations."

The Frenchman who first succeeded in winning the friendship of the Five Nations was Robert Cavelier, Sieur de La Salle. In 1669, La Salle persuaded the Five Nations to provide him with guides for explorations over the Niagara portage to Lake Erie and down the Pennsylvania creeks to the Ohio River.

Ten years later, La Salle won the Five Nations' consent to build a fort on the bluff of Lake Ontario at the mouth of the Niagara Gorge and to construct a shipyard on the upper Niagara River.

Between January and May of 1679, La Salle's helpers built the sailing ship *Griffon,* on the shore of Cayuga Creek, five miles behind the Falls. The *Griffon* was the first sailing ship built on the upper lakes. It carried La Salle and his company west to Green Bay, Wisconsin. This voyage began the explorations that led to La Salle's trip down the Mississippi River in 1681–82 and his claim that the entire area was to become the French territory of Louisiana.

The *Griffon* sank during a storm on its return voyage to Niagara. La Salle's Fort Conde at the Niagara's mouth was burned.

A second French fort built on the same site in 1687 was besieged so thoroughly by the Senecas that 80 of its 125 defenders died. It was abandoned after thirteen months. The Senecas burned it.

In 1721, the Senecas adopted the French trader and spy, Louis

The bateau Marguerite, *on display at Upper Canada Village near Morrisburg, Ontario, is a faithful reproduction of the ships built and used by LaSalle during the 1670's.*

Joncaire, as a "blood brother." They gave him permission to build a trading post at the mouth of the Niagara Gorge, near the site of Lewiston.

Business became so brisk at Joncaire's Magazin Royal that he began nagging the Senecas for permission to build a large stone "House of Peace" on the site of La Salle's fort.

He won their consent in 1726, and the great stone house was started that summer. Its designer was Gaspard Chaussegros de Lery, the engineer who had recently built the stone forts and

(17)

city walls of Quebec. DeLery made the stone walls and floors of the three-story House of Peace so sturdy that they could withstand a cannon siege.

When the building was finished, cannon were smuggled up Lake Ontario from Montreal. Then, each night for a month, a cannon was secretly carried up two flights of stairs to the gun decks behind the dormer windows on the third floor.

The House of Peace became the strongest French fort in the west. France gained control over the Niagara throatway.

Louis Joncaire's son, Chabert, was appointed master of the Niagara portage. He had a wagon road built from the top of the bluff behind Lewiston around the Falls to a boat landing near the site of La Salle's shipyard on Cayuga Creek. Then he imported herds of horses and oxen and developed pasturelands and grain fields for them along the shore of a creek on Lake Erie. He named the creek the River of Horses. The fort beside the boat landing behind the Falls was named Little Niagara.

Chabert hired Seneca women and children to serve as "porters of the Niagara crossing." They carried all the trade goods and furs between the boat landing at Lewiston and the end of the wagon trail on top of the bluff. This mile-long hill is so steep that the porters called it *Duh-jih-heh-oh,* meaning "the place where you crawl on all fours." The women porters carried packs weighing up to 125 pounds strapped to their backs. Husky young farmers from the St. Lawrence Valley and Seneca men and boys became the bullwhackers of the Niagara wagon trains and the herdsmen and farmers of Chabert's ranch on the River of Horses.

(18)

This watercolor by George Heriot, painted before 1790, shows how Buffalo Creek looked when the first Americans settled there. The profile of Fort Erie is visible across the Niagara's headwater at the foot of Lake Erie.

Sir William Johnson

The French and their Indian allies defeated the British-American army commanded by General Braddock and Colonel George Washington near the site of Pittsburgh on July 9, 1755. Most of the cannon captured in the battle were hauled and boated to Fort Niagara to strengthen the defense system there.

The victory over Braddock convinced many of the Six Nations' warriors, as well as Indian tribes in the midwest and south, that France would win a complete victory over Great Britain. The Indians captured hundreds of men, women, and children on plunder raids along the New York, Pennsylvania, and Virginia frontier and brought many of them to Fort Niagara. Some were sold as slaves. Others were used as house servants, cooks, and gardeners by the French families at the Fort.

An expedition of four thousand British regulars, colonial volunteers, and Indians besieged Fort Niagara during July, 1759. Brigadier General John Prideaux was commander of the expedition. Sir William Johnson, the British "agent to the North American Indians," was in charge of the thousand Indian allies. When a British siege gun exploded on the evening of July 20, killing General Prideaux, Sir William Johnson became commander.

On the morning of July 24, a French army of six hundred soldiers and boatmen and fifteen hundred Indians from the upper lakes attacked the British. But Sir William Johnson's scouts had warned him in time to have log and brush barricades built across the trail a mile up the Niagara. The forest there was called La Belle Famille ("the beautiful family"). Colonial soldiers and Six Nations warriors ambushed the French at La Belle Famille and, in a two-hour battle, killed hundreds of them.

Fort Niagara surrendered to Sir William Johnson on July 25.

Great Britain's thirty-six-year reign over both shores of the Niagara was bloodier than the thirty-nine-year reign by New France.

In 1763, Indian tribes on the upper Great Lakes joined Chief Pontiac in a revolt against "British slavery." The Indians captured all the British forts in the west except Pittsburgh, Detroit, and Niagara. Fort Niagara became the British lifeline for routing troops and supplies to the besieged garrison at Detroit.

Naturally, Pontiac tried to persuade Six Nations warriors to revolt, too. Many of the Senecas, Oneidas, and Cayugas did.

On September 14, 1763, Pontiac's Seneca allies ambushed a

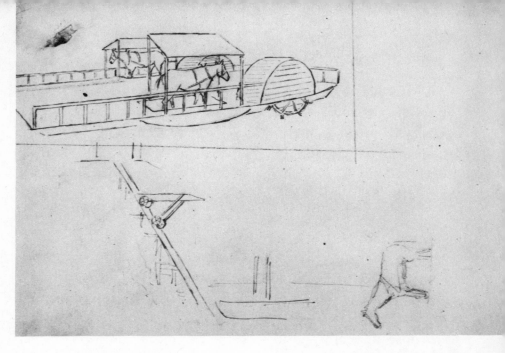

These rough sketches of a horsepowered ferryboat (top) and of a horse-powered elevator (bottom) show the ingenious uses of horsepower made by Niagarans before the invention of the steam engine. The railroad built up Crawl-on-All-Fours by Captain Montresor in 1764 probably looked like the bottom sketch.

British wagon train at Devil's Hole, three miles below the Falls. They killed and scalped eighty-eight wagonmen and soldiers, stole the supplies and horses, and pushed the wagons into the gorge.

Thousands of British and colonial troops assembled at Fort Niagara during the spring and summer of 1764 for the campaign to end the Pontiac War. They built a chain of blockhouse forts across the portage. The last fort in the chain, perched on a bluff above the Lake Erie shore, was named Fort Erie.

During the same months, Captain John Montresor, chief engineer of the British armies in North America, designed and supervised the construction of a railroad, operated by balanced weights, that carried trade goods and supplies over the Crawl-on-All-Fours Hill. This was the first railroad built in North America.

Several of the officers assigned to the Niagara garrison between 1765 and 1775 had served with British regiments in India. They were familiar with the water buffalo used as plow animals in the Orient. So they gave the same name to the American bison. Perhaps they were responsible for changing the name of the River of Horses to Buffalo Creek. Nobody really knows how or why the name was changed. It occurred between 1760 and 1775. It was an important change because, in 1808, Buffalo Creek gave its name to the village that became the second largest city in New York State.

After the American rebels wrote their Declaration of Independence in the summer of 1776 and reorganized the Thirteen Colonies into the United States of America, Fort Niagara became a stronghold for the Loyalists.

The son of Sir William Johnson along with Captain John Butler formed regiments of Royal Rangers at Niagara. Joseph Brant and other Six Nations leaders organized corps of warriors to fight for the king. The Rangers and Indians terrorized the New York and Pennsylvania frontiers. The massacres of Wyoming, Cherry Valley, German Flats, and Schoharie were all committed by Loyalists out of Niagara.

(23)

Joseph Brant

Butler Barracks, built in 1776-77 for Butler's Rangers, was the first building on the Upper Canada shore of the Niagara's mouth.

The Loyalist terror raids forced General George Washington to put one third of all the American armies under the command of Generals Clinton and Sullivan for a campaign to wipe out the Six Nations and capture Fort Niagara. During the summer and fall of 1779, the Clinton-Sullivan expedition did destroy most of the Six Nations' strongholds in central and western New York. But it failed to capture Fort Niagara.

Thousands of Indians fled to the Niagara. Hundreds died from starvation and disease during "the great starving time" that winter.

The next spring General Frederick Haldimand, governor-general of Canada, ordered the Indians and Rangers to prepare gardens and farms along the Niagara shore. He offered them tracts of land for homesteads where they might live until "the

Sir Frederick Haldimand

rebellion is crushed and you can return to your homes in the Colonies." He called this program the Niagara Plan of Edible Annex.

When the American Revolution ended in 1783, more than ten thousand Loyalists and Indian refugees were living on the Niagara shores.

Great Britain refused to surrender any part of the Niagara to the United States. General Haldimand had developed a plan to settle other Loyalist refugees and thousands of Scottish and Welsh along the Ontario-Niagara shore. He planned a new royal province to be called Upper Canada.

That is why the Americans were barred from using the Great Lakes for their migrations to the west. Instead, their wagon trains jangled down toward Pittsburgh and the "big floatway" of the Ohio. When their new government became strong enough, they resolved, Niagara would be conquered. Then the Great Lakes would become an American throughway.

Land of Promise

Thousands of families living in the Thirteen Colonies preferred the established British system of government to the new, untried system of the United States. During and after the Revolution these people fled to Canada. The British province of Upper Canada provided them with a new homeland. The first capital of Upper Canada was the village of Newark (now Niagara-on-the-Lake), across the Niagara River from Fort Niagara.

The migrations up the St. Lawrence River to Upper Canada began during the 1780's. The journey was as brave an undertaking as that which Americans were making by wagon train, pack pony, and flatboat into Kentucky, Ohio, Indiana, and Tennessee during the same years.

Upper Canada, too, was virgin wilderness. The only settlements west of Montreal clustered around the forts of Frontenac, Toronto, Niagara, and Detroit. The forests had to be chopped down and burned before crops could be planted. Rattlesnakes, copperheads, bears, and bobcats were a summer-long menace, and wolves came down from the northlands during the fall and winter. There were no roads. When Lake Ontario and the rivers froze, snowshoes and sleds became the only means of transportation.

(27)

This scene, painted by James Peachey during the 1790's, shows the first buildings of Newark, Upper Canada's first capital, in foreground and the structures of Fort Niagara across the Niagara's mouth on Lake Erie.

The first session of Upper Canada's Parliament began in Newark on September 17, 1792. The delegates could grin proudly at the new farms and new villages all along Ontario's shore. Kingston had grown on the ruins of the French Fort Frontenac. York was building near the Indian village and fort the French had called Toronto. The soil and climate behind Burlington Bay, at the west end of Ontario, were successfully producing crops of peaches and grapes.

But the greatest changes in all Upper Canada were occurring along the Niagara. So many farms had been started atop the gorge that grain mills and sawmills, cheese factories and woolen mills clanked and snarled in the new villages of Queenston and Chippawa. A broad dirt road over the ridge enabled covered wagons to deliver supplies between the Newark and Chippawa boat docks in eight hours.

A day's horseback ride west from the Falls, the Seneca, Mohawk, and Cayuga Indian families who had chosen to live under the king's protection were developing farms and villages in the Grand River valley. In 1784, George III gave them a tract twelve miles wide from Lake Erie to the headwaters of the Grand. The village of Brantford, named for Joseph Brant, was growing near the church that the king had ordered built for them.

A set of laws that would guarantee equal rights for all the residents of Upper Canada was the greatest challenge confronting the first parliament. The members debated for three months.

They reached agreement about the problem of human slavery. The tiny kingdom of Denmark was the only nation on earth that had passed a law forbidding the enslavement of one human being by another. Parliament agreed with the Danes and voted to outlaw slavery in Upper Canada.

Gossip about the law against slavery soon reached the United States. Most Americans in the northern states favored it. Before 1810, laws against slavery were adopted in the states north of the Ohio and Potomac rivers. But the invention of the cotton gin in 1793 and the need for field laborers to tend the tobacco and rice crops had prompted most planters and politicians south of the Potomac and Ohio rivers to advocate a system of human slavery.

(29)

King George III ordered the construction of this royal chapel in 1785 for the loyal Mohawks and other Iroquois who fled to Niagara during the American Revolution. Joseph Brant is buried here. Mohawk Chapel stands on the outskirts of Brantford, Ontario.

Blacks in the United States began to plot methods and routes for escaping to Upper Canada. The Niagara River was the easiest place to cross into "the Land of Promise."

The first blacks who braved the freedom road crossed the Upper Niagara during 1795. They were escorted to one of the Indian villages in the Grand River valley. The chiefs gave them a formal welcome and ruled that they were to be given sections of land for developing farms.

Records kept by the government of Upper Canada during the War of 1812 show that forty of the soldiers who fought for Upper Canada were "Negroes living on the Grand River Reservation." During the 1838–39 Patriots' War in Canada, more than three hundred blacks volunteered and served with the Upper Canada militia. One all-black company was commanded by a Captain John Clench.

So many slaves fled toward the Land of Promise during the 1820's and 1830's that plantation owners hired slave catchers to seize any black boarding the trans-Niagara ferryboats at Lewiston, Black Rock, and Buffalo. The plantation owners offered rewards of one thousand dollars for the capture and return to the South of a "healthy Negro."

After the slave catchers made the ferry ride too risky, the

This painting by C. W. Simpson shows an outdoor session of Upper Canada's first Parliament at Newark's Navy Hall late in the summer of 1792.

refugees were forced to swim the river or attempt to float across Lake Ontario or Lake Erie on rafts. On August 10, 1823, the Canadian steamer, *Chief Justice Robinson*, picked up a black man floating on a plank farm-gate twelve miles from shore in Lake Ontario. Too exhausted to swim away, the man refused to come aboard the ship until an officer assured him that it was Canadian. Then he climbed the rope ladder, fell to his knees on the deck and prayed. "Thank you, Lord, for delivering me to Canaan!"

Many of the songs known as spirituals were composed and first sung by black slaves. Most scholars of America's folk music believe that biblical references such as "the promised land" and "land of Canaan" mentioned in some of these songs referred to Upper Canada, and that "River Jordan" was often used as a code name for the Niagara.

By 1820, many white people were helping slaves to escape and were devising methods to smuggle them into Upper Canada. The network of hiding places that was developed and the wagons and carts used for smuggling were called the Underground Railroad. The Quakers of Pennsylvania and Ohio and the Congregationalists of New England were the first organizers of the Underground Railroad. Later, abolitionist societies raised funds to expand the system and to provide homes and money for blacks who reached Upper Canada.

One type of vehicle that became a common sight along the American bank of the Niagara after 1830 was a wagon with a big box seat on the front end. The seat was completely enclosed, like a chest standing on its side. When questioned about the "big seat," the wagon driver would grumpily explain that it held tow-ropes, grease buckets, a wagon jack and other tools that might be needed during the "hauls" from his farm to town and back. If a slave catcher called a policeman and demanded that the "tool chest" be opened for examination, the driver would oblige, lift the rear lid, and show the tools inside.

The toolbox had a false back. The secret compartment behind it was large enough to hold an adult slave refugee or two children. Thus the runaways were carried from the Underground Railroad station in a farmer's basement or barn to a home or cave along the Niagara shore. That night a crew of abolitionists would row the refugees across the river to "Canaan."

The Reverend Josiah Henson escaped from slavery to Upper Canada during the 1830's. He became the pastor of a church at Chatham, 150 miles west of Niagara near the Lake Erie shore. His leadership and bravery in the Underground Railroad became so well known that he was invited to Boston, Massachusetts, during the summer of 1850 to address abolitionist meetings. Mrs. Calvin Stowe spent many hours that summer interviewing the Reverend Henson about his life story. Two years later, Mrs. Stowe's famous book, *Uncle Tom's Cabin,* was published. It is believed that Harriet Beecher Stowe modeled the character Uncle Tom after Reverend Henson.

Historians believe that more than seventy-five thousand black Americans escaped to Upper Canada during the sixty-eight years between 1795 and 1863. This era when the Niagara served as the gateway to the Land of Promise is one of the most important and most meaningful in its saga.

Dread Frontier

Great Britain signed a new treaty with the United States during 1794. It stated that Upper Canada would abandon the forts on the eastern shore of the Great Lakes and the Niagara by June 1, 1796. John Jay, chief justice of the United States, headed the American delegation that arranged the treaty. So the treaty is called Jay's Treaty.

The terms of the treaty angered many congressmen, especially those from the South and West. They charged that British agents and army officers were advising and arming the Indians of Ohio, Indiana, and Kentucky and urging them to fight against the Americans. "Jay's Treaty," the congressmen stormed, "doesn't do anything about that!"

Great Britain and France were deadlocked in the Napoleonic wars. Each nation had announced that it was blockading the other's seaports and that all neutral nations were forbidden to trade with "the enemy." Both French and British fighting ships were stopping American merchant ships on the high seas, searching them, and kidnapping some of the crewmen.

Jay's Treaty, the congressmen pointed out, did nothing to end this "piracy" either. They believed that there was sure to be another war with Great Britain, and perhaps with France, too.

John Jay

After debating Jay's Treaty for almost two years, they finally approved it, but by a majority of only three votes.

These fears and misunderstandings were responsible for the bloodiest years in the Niagara's history.

The British kept the promises given in Jay's Treaty. Fort Niagara was abandoned on June 1, 1796. So were the portage road, the east-shore blockhouses, and Captain Montresor's railroad up Crawl-on-All-Fours.

But Upper Canada built a larger, stronger fort named Fort George on the bluff behind Newark. Its cannon were supposed to be powerful enough to destroy Fort Niagara within an hour. Upper Canada also had the advantage in boat traffic in the upper Niagara. The rapids there were too powerful for a sailing ship

This is the view of the Niagara's mouth that the Americans saw when they reached Fort Niagara in 1796. Upper Canada's Fort George is up-river at left. The buildings of Newark are at right.

to navigate upstream. The schooners and brigs had to be towed. But the towpath was on the Upper Canada shore; its terminals were protected by the cannon of Fort Erie and Fort Chippawa.

The British did not, of course, turn over any of the Lake Ontario and upper lakes warships to the United States. Strong fleets had been on patrol since the Pontiac War. The Navy yards were at Newark and Kingston on Lake Ontario and at Fort Erie and the Detroit River on the upper lakes.

Less than a hundred American soldiers were sent out to occupy Fort Niagara in 1796. The only route to the Niagara from the United States used the Mohawk River to the site of Rome, portaged to Lake Oneida, then followed the rocky Oswego River down to Fort Oswego on Lake Ontario. From there, it was a two-hundred-mile sail and row uplake to the Niagara.

The United States Navy built only two small ships on the Great Lakes between 1797 and 1812. One patrolled the upper lakes between Buffalo Creek and Mackinac Island. The other, a brig, patrolled Ontario between Niagara and the Thousand Islands.

The first American road across western New York bypassed the Niagara. It was chopped through the forests from the Genesee River, near the site of Rochester, to the village of Batavia, and across the glacial ridge to the shore of Lake Erie near Buffalo Creek.

In 1808 the villagers on the shore of Buffalo Creek voted down the suggestion to name their community "New Amsterdam." They insisted that it be called Buffalo. Everybody had forgotten that the French name of this creek was the River of Horses.

By that time hundreds of Americans had settled along the eastern shore of the Niagara, too. New mills manufactured rope from wild hemp and tar. Canals were dug in from the upper rapids to provide waterpower. An important trade in salt developed. The "sacred lake" of the Onondaga Indians near the site of Syracuse was rich in salt. Thousands of tons of Onondaga salt were shipped through Niagara to Pittsburgh.

(37)

*Engraved silver medals that could be worn as necklaces were a favorite
"reward" given to Indian allies during the 150 years of warfare on the
Niagara. Great Britain gave the "Young George III" (top) medal to friendly
chiefs after the Pontiac Rebellion. The newly formed United States gave
the "George Washington Indian Chief Medal" (bottom left and right) to
Indian delegates who signed a peace treaty with the United States in 1792.*

Congressmen from the Kentucky-Ohio West and the South were again demanding that the United States declare war against Great Britain. Henry Clay of Kentucky and John C. Calhoun of South Carolina became known as "The War Hawks." They believed that most Canadians wanted to join the United States. They said that an army sent to the Niagara could quickly conquer all of Canada.

After angry arguments, first the House of Representatives and finally the Senate approved the declaration of war. President Madison announced a state of war on June 19, 1812. There were street riots in New York and other coastal cities. The New Englanders were angriest of all and nicknamed the war "Mr. Madison's War."

By midsummer, 7,000 American soldiers were in camp on the Niagara. But 5,200 were New York militiamen who had enlisted for only six months.

Upper Canada had fewer than 3,000 soldiers, but they were better trained and had more Indian allies than the Americans. During August, Upper Canadians and Indians captured Detroit, the 2,000 American troops defending it, and the United States Navy's only ship on the upper lakes.

Most of the Detroit prisoners were marched along the Upper Canada shore of the Niagara River toward the Montreal prison camps. But no effort to rescue them was ordered by the officers commanding the 7,000 Americans on the east shore.

On October 13 the American officers finally ordered a dawn attack against the Upper Canada entrenchment at Queenston.

The Canadian artillery barrage sank 25 boats and killed more

Artist W. H. Bartlett sketched this view of the lower Niagara during the 1830's. At left is a monument to Sir Isaac Brock, the "Victor of Detroit," who was killed at Queenston.

than 100 Americans. But 1,000 survived the rowboat trip. They battled up the Queenston ridge and captured the gun batteries on top. General Isaac Brock, the "Victor of Detroit," was killed while leading a charge against them.

When the American commanders ordered the rest of the New York militiamen to cross the Niagara and reinforce their besieged comrades on Queenston Heights, the militiamen refused to enter the boats. They had "joined up," their spokesmen said, "to defend the Sovereign State of New York. We aren't supposed to invade another country."

More than 3,000 militiamen sat on the rocks near Lewiston and watched while the Americans on Queenston Heights fought off a second and third Canadian charge. But by dusk, they had run out of ammunition. They surrendered.

A few moments after the surrender, two Indians from the Grand River reservation attempted to tomahawk the young lieutenant colonel who commanded the Americans on the heights. An Upper Canada officer slashed the Indians down with his sword. The lieutenant colonel was Winfield Scott who became, historians agree, the greatest American military genius between George Washington and Robert E. Lee.

American preparations for the 1813 campaign centered at Sackets Harbor at the eastern end of Lake Ontario and at Erie, Pennsylvania. At both places, hundreds of veteran shipbuilders were marched in to develop shipyards and build fleets of United States Navy warships.

A brilliant young Navy veteran from Rhode Island was appointed to command the American fleet on the upper lakes. His name was Oliver Hazard Perry.

A brigadier general who was famous as one of the greatest explorers of the American Far West was appointed to command the army assembling at Sackets Harbor. His name was Zebulon Pike. (A majestic mountain he had discovered in Colorado in 1806 was named Pike's Peak in his honor. The tallest cliff on the Iowa shore of the upper Mississippi was also named Pike's Peak because of the important explorations he made there during 1804–5.)

Four of the ships needed for Commander Perry's fleet on the upper lakes were in the American harbor at Black Rock, behind Niagara Falls. But they could not be towed up into Lake Erie until Forts Chippewa and Erie were captured.

General Pike and his men were ordered to attack York (now Toronto), the capital of Upper Canada, en route to Niagara. Pike was killed by the explosion of the powder magazine at York's principal fort. York was pillaged and most of the city was burned. (The capture of Washington, D.C., by British troops, effected August 25, 1814, and the burning of the United States Capitol and the White House were ordered by the British government as revenge for the burning of York and Newark.)

American troops captured all of the Upper Canada forts on the Niagara during May 27–29, 1813. The warships trapped at Black Rock were towed out to Lake Erie, and sailed west to join the ships being launched at Erie.

On September 10, Commander Perry's fleet attacked the Upper Canada fleet at Put-in-Bay, off Sandusky, Ohio. That evening, Perry wrote his famous victory message, beginning, "We have met the enemy and they are ours. . . ." The Battle of Lake Erie gave the United States control of the upper lakes.

However, bad generalship plagued the American Army on the Niagara. Two expeditions against the Upper Canada forces entrenched on Burlington Heights were ambushed; more than 600 men were captured.

That fall, most of the American troops were ordered to join

an expedition against Montreal. It was a bumbling failure.

The Upper Canadian commanders hurried 1,000 soldiers back to Niagara for a winter campaign.

The brigadier general who had succeeded to the American command on the Niagara was a militiaman with poor training and no battle experience. On the night of December 10, with snow threatening and the temperature dropping toward zero, he warned all Canadians in Newark to abandon their homes. At 10 P.M., he ordered the eighty homes of Newark set afire, the powder magazines at Fort George blown up, and a retreat across the river to Fort Niagara. The next day he turned the command of Fort Niagara over to an artillery captain and fled east toward Albany.

Revenge came quickly. Boats with muffled oars carried 600 Canadians across the Niagara between 1 and 2 A.M. on December 18. They were under orders to capture Fort Niagara "by the bayonet and without quarter." They did.

That dawn, another detachment of 500 captured Lewiston and the portage road and by late afternoon was setting fire to the village of Black Rock and its shipyards.

A few days later, Buffalo was captured after a fifteen-minute battle. It, too, was burned to the ground.

The Upper Canadians held Fort Niagara and most of the Niagara Gorge during the last year of the war.

Major General Jacob Brown and Winfield Scott, promoted to brigadier general, led 4,500 United States Army regulars into Buffalo during March, 1814. They devoted the next three months to intensive battle drills.

Winfield Scott in 1814.

Winfield Scott led the attack that recaptured Fort Erie on July 3. The next day — Independence Day — Scott's 1,300 regulars defeated 2,100 Canadians at the Battle of Chippawa. The victory was so thorough that the War Department ordered the gray and gold uniform worn by Scott's troops that day to become the standard uniform of the cadet corps at the new United States Military Academy at West Point. (The battle dress of the Chippawa victors is still the cadet uniform at West Point.)

The grimmest battle of the War of 1812 was fought at Lundy's Lane in Upper Canada, within two miles of Niagara Falls, on July 25, 1814. The armies were evenly matched, with approximately 3,000 on each side. The battle raged from sunset until midnight. Each army lost almost a third of its men: 860 for the Americans; 878 for the Canadians. Generals Brown and Scott were wounded. So was the Canadian commander, General Gordon Drummond.

Lundy's Lane was the high tide of the American efforts to conquer Upper Canada. The peace treaty signed on Christmas Eve, 1814, restored the international boundary line to its prewar route — down the center of the Niagara River.

Three-and-a-half years later, the Rush-Bagot Treaty ended the race to build fighting ships on the Great Lakes by stipulating that both Great Britain and the United States would limit naval forces to patrol vessels.

Then both Canada and the United States concentrated on the challenge to build ship routes around Niagara Falls.

The Canawlers

The War of 1812 gave both Canada and the United States freedom of travel through Niagara and the Great Lakes. The western frontier moved rapidly across the prairies toward the Rocky Mountains. The "big digs" that began on both shores of the Niagara a few years after the War of 1812 were important to both the American and Canadian rush to the Far West. Between 1817 and 1825, the Americans built the Erie Canal and launched Buffalo on its career toward becoming the second largest city in New York State. Between 1823 and 1828, Upper Canada built the Welland Canal that lifted ships over the Niagara's ridge.

DeWitt Clinton was the son of one of the colonial officers who helped win the Battle of La Belle Famille and capture Fort Niagara in 1760. Clinton became the most outspoken champion for a ship canal that would connect Lake Erie with the Mohawk and Hudson rivers. He renewed his campaign for a Grand Erie Canal when the War of 1812 ended. The bill to finance "Clinton's Ditch," as it was called, passed the New York legislature in 1817.

The ancient throughway that had been plowed across western and central New York by the glacial melt-off made the task much simpler. Two of the major problems were: how to get the canal

The Welland Canal, built during the 1820's, enabled ships to sail past the Falls between the "upper" and "lower" Great Lakes.

up the Niagara ridge to Lake Erie, and where to locate the Lake Erie terminal.

Engineers decided that the best way to get the canal up the ridge was to blast out a series of big steps twenty miles east of Niagara Falls. The locks built into these steps floated the canalboats up or down the 326-foot ridge. The city that grew around the locks was called Lockport.

An angry argument developed between Buffalo and Black Rock. Both villages wanted to become the Lake Erie terminal of the canal. Black Rock was on the upper Niagara. Buffalo was closer to the lakeshore. But Buffalo did not have a harbor, and a huge sandbar had formed across the mouth of Buffalo Creek.

The Buffalonians contributed funds to dredge the creek and build breakwaters and piers on the Lake Erie shore. So their village became the western terminal of the canal. In 1821 only 120 vessels docked at Buffalo; in 1825, the year the Canal opened, 972 ships used the port of Buffalo.

Both the Erie and the Welland were tiny waterways. The channel of the Erie was only four feet deep. Steamboats could not use it because it was too shallow for paddlewheels. The Welland was eight feet deep. Its locks were only 22 feet wide and 110 feet long.

The canalboat became the fashionable method for travel across New York as well as through the Welland. A canalboat was long and narrow, like a barge. It was hauled by a rope attached to a team of mules or horses that walked along the towpath on the canal shore. The crewmen of the boats and the teamsters were nicknamed "canawlers." By 1845 there were five thousand canawlers, mostly teen-agers, working on the Erie.

The ports above and below Niagara Falls became big ship-building centers, too. Noah Brown, the navy-yard veteran who built Commander Perry's ships at Erie, Pennsylvania, built the first steamboat on the upper Great Lakes at Black Rock during

John A. Roebling, designer of the Brooklyn Bridge, built the first rail-road-and-carriage suspension bridge across the Niagara's gorge during 1854-55. Prints of the bridge and Falls, like this one, became the cherished parlor-picture in thousands of American homes.

1818. The Indian name for a steamboat was "Ship-that-walks-on-the-water." So Brown named his steamboat *Walk-On-the-Water.*

Newark, Fort Erie, and Port Colborne all became major ship-building centers for Upper Canada's schooners, snows, brigs, steamboats, and canalboats.

(49)

The first steam railroads hammered into Buffalo and the Niagara Gorge during the 1840's. Hundreds of the canawlers decided there was a brighter future in railroading.

Theodore DeHone Judah was an assistant engineer for the construction of the first railroad down the Niagara Gorge to Lockport. He went to California in 1854, built the first railroad on the Pacific coast, then discovered the route for the first transcontinental railroad across the Sierras and became its chief engineer.

Samuel B. Reed, superintendent of construction for the eastern end of the first transcontinental railroad, the Union Pacific, had been a survey engineer on the Erie Canal.

Wells, Fargo & Company, the most famous operator of stagecoaches in the Far West, began as a parcel-post delivery service on the canalboats between Buffalo and Albany.

The canals and the railroads made Niagara Falls the most popular tourist center in the New World. A boat or train journey to "see the wondrous cataract" became a holiday excursion that most couples could afford "at least once." And if it was "once," it was usually the honeymoon trip.

Honeymooners' Paradise

More than two thousand years ago, a philosopher named Antipater wrote a description of what he considered to be the world's most remarkable buildings and works of art. The title of his book, *The Seven Wonders of the World,* became more popular than the book itself. By 1700, Niagara Falls was being called one of the seven wonders of the world.

Scientists from Sweden, Great Britain, France, and Holland made the dangerous journey through the wilderness to measure the height of the Falls, examine the types of rocks, and study the animals, snakes, and birds in the gorge.

Benjamin Franklin told a tall story about the Falls in 1765. He blandly assured the editors of a London newspaper that "the grand leap of the Whale up the Fall of Niagara is esteemed, by all who have seen it, as one of the finest spectacles in Nature."

Oliver Goldsmith, the English poet, described how "Niagara stuns with thundering sound" in his poem *The Traveler*.

John James Audubon, the greatest American painter of birds and animals, became so awestruck by the Falls and gorge that he wrote, "All the pictures you may see, all the descriptions you may read of these mighty falls, can only produce in your mind

(51)

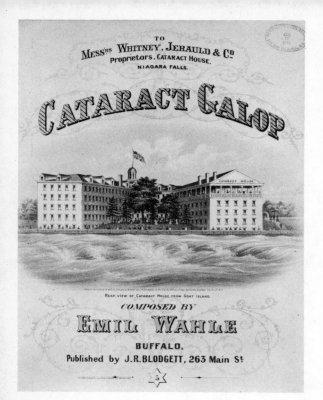

TO
MESS^{RS} WHITNEY, JERAULD & C^O
Proprietors, CATARACT HOUSE.
NIAGARA FALLS.

CATARACT GALOP

REAR VIEW OF CATARACT HOUSE FROM GOAT ISLAND.
COMPOSED BY
EMIL WAHLE
BUFFALO,
Published by J.R.BLODGETT, 263 Main St

*Music composers as well as poets and paint-
ers and authors praised the "majestic wonders of Niagara." This is the title page of
Emil Wahle's Cataract Galop, a dance tune
dedicated to the proprietors of the Cataract
House.*

the faint glimmer of the glowworm compared with the over-
powering glory of the meridian sun."

General Lafayette spent two days at the Falls and in the gorge
during June, 1825, and was so enchanted that he seriously considered buying Goat Island as "my vacation home in America."
(The price then being asked for Goat Island was one thousand
dollars.)

Mrs. Frances Trollope, an English authoress, was so overcome
by her first view of the Falls in 1831 that, she wrote, "I trembled
like a fool, and my girls clung to me, trembling, too . . . but with
faces beaming with delight."

(52)

Artists became fascinated by "the many moods of Niagara" and tried to depict all of them. By the 1830's, every art museum in Europe owned at least one "Niagara painting," and in parlors and inns and steamboat salons from New Orleans to Moscow, there were hand-tinted prints of "The Great Cataract" — in rainbowed sunlight, by starlight, ice-sheathed, or during a thunderstorm.

All of this artistic publicity made the Falls an essential for

W. H. Bartlett painted this scene of the Niagara's gorge during the 1830's.

holiday adventures when canalboat, steamship, and rail transportation became available.

Visitors before 1840 usually spent three days on a carriage or coach trip up one side of the gorge and down the other. Battle scars from the War of 1812 could still be seen on trees and hillsides. A rickety tree ladder was the only way to reach the giant rocks at the foot of the Falls. Another tree ladder wobbled down the gorge cliff to Devil's Hole.

There were military drills and afternoon band concerts at Fort Niagara and Fort George, plus the tingling realization that the guns across the river were trained on you.

The steamboat ride down Lake Erie from Cleveland cost $5.00. So did the trip from Newark to Kingston. The canalboat fare between Buffalo and Schenectady was $6.50 — including meals and a bunk.

The first steamboat offering the thrill of a ride through the upper gorge to the foot of the Falls was built in 1846. The craft, like all her successors, carried the name *Maid of the Mist*.

The catwalk tour, in raincoats, to the Cave of the Winds beneath the Falls was pioneered during the 1850's.

Samuel L. Clemens — Mark Twain — bought a partnership in a Buffalo newspaper in 1869. He soon wearied of it and sold out. But during the year he was on the Niagara, he wrote several tongue-in-cheek articles about the tourist attractions of the Falls. One of them went like this:

When you have examined the stupendous Horseshoe Fall till you are satisfied you cannot improve on it, you return

(54)

to America by the new Suspension Bridge, and follow up the bank to where they exhibit the Cave of the Winds. . . . Such a mad storming, roaring, bellowing of warring wind and water never crazed my ears before. I bent my head and seemed to receive the Atlantic on my back. The world seemed going to destruction. I could not see anything, the flood poured down so savagely.

I raised my head, with open mouth, and most of the American cataract went down my throat. If I had sprung a leak now I had been lost. And at this moment, I discovered that the bridge had ceased, and we must now trust for a foothold to the slippery and precipitious rocks. I never was so scared before and survived it.

But we got through at last, and emerged into the open day, where we could stand in front of the laced and frothy and seething world of descending water and look at it. When I saw how much of it there was, and how fearfully in earnest it was, I was sorry I had gone behind it.

One discreet rule adopted by all the proprietors of Falls hotels and boarding houses may have been responsible for the Niagara's reputation as "the honeymooners' paradise." The rule was so simple it didn't have to be put on bulletin boards. It was: *Don't pester the guests*.

There were no social directors or guided tours or parlor games or evening lectures or magic shows. There were not even scheduled hours for meals. Guests could get up when they wanted to, eat when they wanted to, and do what they wanted to do. And

The Queen's Royal Niagara Hotel was one of the posh resorts for Niagara honeymooners during the 1860's.

everybody from the bellhops to the desk clerk with the waxed moustache had strict orders to act as though the guests were always right.

So by the time the British poet Oscar Wilde toured the United States in order to write a book of witty insults about Americans, he could truthfully observe, "Every American bride is taken to Niagara Falls."

Niagara's popularity lured the notoriety seekers, too. Their efforts to defy the power of Niagara's torrent began in 1859 when a young Frenchman announced that he would walk across the gorge on a tightrope.

The Daredevils

Like many small boys in France — or anywhere else — Jean François Gravelet tried to walk along the top of the village fences. It was easy. He tried walking across his mother's clothesline — and succeeded. By 1850, he was a popular tightrope walker and trapeze performer with a circus. He chose the stage name of the Great Blondin because it sounded like Blondel, the French troubador and folk hero who helped rescue King Richard the Lionhearted from prison.

Jean Gravelet realized that he could become the world's most famous tightrope walker if he succeeded in walking across the Niagara Falls Gorge.

The Niagara's popularity as a honeymoon and vacation place had lured hundreds of gift shops, fortune-telling tents, merry-go-rounds, sharpshooter galleries and games of chance to the portage road. One of the largest was called White's Pleasure Ground, a half mile below the Falls. Gravelet contracted to anchor the American end of his tightrope at White's Pleasure Ground. Hundreds of seats were built along the gorge brink near the anchoring places. Gravelet and the Pleasure Ground owners were to share the profits from the seat rentals.

The announcement that a walk across the gorge would be at-

The Great Blondin crossing the Falls' gorge on a tightrope in 1859.

tempted on June 30, 1859, brought thousands of visitors. Professional gamblers offered four silver dollars for one that Gravelet would never make it. Armed guards were stationed at each end of the cable.

Gravelet, dressed in scarlet trunks and carrying a balancing pole thirty-eight feet long, began the walk at four o'clock that afternoon. He strolled a hundred feet out, sat down, lay on his back, then stood up on one foot, bowed to the crowd and sauntered on towards the Canadian shore.

The *Maid of the Mist* puffed upriver until it was directly beneath the cable. Gravelet stopped again, pulled a cord out of his trunks, and lowered it to the deck of the *Maid of the Mist*.

The ship's captain tied a bottle of root beer onto the cord. Gravelet hauled the bottle up, saluted the crowds on both shores, and took a long, slow drink. Then he lowered the bottle back to the steamboat and walked on to Canada. The whole trip took eighteen minutes.

Just before five o'clock, Gravelet stepped up on the cable again. He wanted to show how quickly the walk could be taken, so he did not stop for tricks. The thirteen-hundred-foot journey took seven minutes.

The eyestrain, gasps, and swooning spells the Great Blondin caused that summer and fall gave the Niagara its most prosperous season. The lithe, thirty-five-year-old Frenchman seemed determined to plunge to his death. He made each performance more difficult than the preceding one. Once, he skipped across the gorge with a potato sack tied over his head. On the next walk, he wore a hat. In midwalk, he held the hat out at arm's

Blondin carrying his manager piggyback on one of his tightrope walks across the Niagara gorge.

length. A marksman aboard the *Maid of the Mist* shot a hole through it.

He crossed the gorge after dark, with colored lamps fastened on each end of the balance pole. He pushed a wheelbarrow across.

But the most spectacular trip of all occurred in mid-August when Gravelet carried his 145-pound manager, Harry Colcord, across the cable, piggyback. The weight made the cable droop at the center. So there was a downhill walk out from the American shore and an uphill climb to the Canadian shore. Colcord climbed down from the shoulder harness seven times during the trip to give Gravelet "a chance to rest and catch his breath." But each time he had to wriggle back up while Gravelt maneuvered the forty-five-pound pole to maintain their balance.

At midstream, Gravelet lost the balance and began to run uphill toward the guy wires extending out from the Canadian shore. He reached the first guy wire and thrust a foot against it to regain balance. The guy wire broke.

Colcord slid out of the harness, gripped Gravelet's waist, and held still while the cable swayed in pendulum arcs. Gravelet maneuvered the balancing pole so deftly that they rode out the sways. Colcord wriggled back up. Gravelet raced to Canada. The trip took twenty-two minutes.

The cable was moved downstream for the summer season of 1860, and suspended across the Whirlpool Rapids. The Prince of Wales — the future King Edward VII — toured Canada and the United States that year. Harry Colcord wrote an invitation to His Royal Highness to be carried piggyback over the Rapids.

During the summer of 1860, the Prince of Wales viewed the "wonders of Niagara Falls." Then, like every other tourist, he posed for a daguerrotype at the Falls' brink. He wore cream-colored breeches, a tall white "beaver," and a gaily-colored waistcoat. He graciously refused the invitation to be carried piggyback across the Niagara gorge by the tightrope walker Blondin.

One of the prince's aides wrote a discreet refusal. But the prince and his party did carriage down to watch one of Gravelet's crossings.

Abraham Lincoln visited the Falls that year, too. Gravelet did not put on a performance for Mr. Lincoln.

The Civil War ended Niagara performances by the Great Blondin. Great Britain was friendly to the Confederacy. The Union feared invasions across the Niagara by Canadian troops or Rebel sympathizers — perhaps both. Jean François Gravelet went to England and demonstrated his high-wire skills before Queen Victoria. He earned a fortune, won many medals, and died in bed in 1897.

In 1865, after the Civil War ended, the wire walks were renewed. American, Canadian, and Italian gymnasts made the trips summer after summer. Mark Twain became so bored by the exhibitions that he wrote a series of articles for his Buffalo newspaper, pretending that he was an Irish reporter, named Michael J. Murphy, marooned "220 feet above the river," on a velocipede and "starving to death without an umbrella," but worst of all, "I was to have been married today!" By the late 1870's, another form of daredevil show made the wire walks unprofitable.

The craze grew to shoot the Whirlpool Rapids while sealed inside a barrel. One skinny barrelmaker named Carlisle Graham survived five such trips. Several men, and at least one woman, died from suffocation or were drowned when the barrels broke.

In October, 1901, a forty-three-year-old schoolteacher named Annie Edson Taylor rode a barrel over the Horseshoe Falls. She had designed a padded steel-bound barrel with a blacksmith's

Mrs. Anna Edson Taylor and what is probably a replica of the barrel in which she rode over the Falls in October, 1901.

anvil strapped on the bottom. Although she announced her intentions weeks in advance and made a test run of the barrel, no effort was made to halt what was believed to be her certain suicide.

The ride began from Grass Island, a mile above the Falls, at about 3:30 P.M. Thousands of curious onlookers stood by. Again, the gamblers were alert. They offered even money that the barrel would swirl toward one of the shores and shatter against the boulders at the foot of the Falls. But the spinning barrel held to the center of the rapids, hurtled end over end into the deep pool below the Horseshoe Falls, bobbed up and floated serenely toward the Canadian shore.

Seventeen minutes after the plunge, rescuers pulled the barrel ashore and removed the lid. Mrs. Taylor stood up, waved to the crowds, and fainted.

Barrel jumps over the Falls continued until the 1940's. Several fame seekers were killed. Then laws were passed declaring Falls jumps, tight-rope walks, swims through the rapids, and similar daredevil challenges of Niagara to be "public nuisances."

The most amazing Falls jump ever reported was made during the afternoon of July 9, 1960, by a seven-year-old boy. Roger Woodward and his seventeen-year-old sister, Deanne, went fishing with Jim Honeycutt, a family friend, on the Niagara River behind the Falls. The motor of the Honeycutt boat failed. Honeycutt ordered Deanne and Roger to put on life jackets as he tried desperately to row the craft to shore. But the current pulled the craft into the rapids. It hit rocks and sank.

Deanne Woodward was swept toward the shore of Goat Island and rescued by onlookers. Honeycutt and Roger were whirled over the Falls.

Honeycutt was killed, but Roger survived the 161-foot drop and the crushing force of the whirlpools. He was rescued by the crew of the *Maid of the Mist*. Physicians reported that he had received "only a few bruises and scratches."

Becoming Good Neighbors

There were a good many reasons, when the War of 1812 ended, for the United States and Canada to go on being enemies. Between 1812 and 1815 both Canada and the United States lost thousands of men and suffered greatly from the plunders and town burnings of the War of 1812.

The Rush-Bagot Agreement, signed during April, 1818, was a great and important step toward becoming Good Neighbors. The frontier between the United States and Canada is more than three thousand miles long. Almost half of it runs along the St. Lawrence River and the Great Lakes. So the Rush-Bagot Agreement to stop building big fleets of warships on the Great Lakes was a major step toward peace.

But there was grave danger of war again on the Niagara in 1837, in 1864, and in 1866. Only good statesmanship prevented serious battles and declarations of war.

The importance of Niagara Falls as a tourist attraction, hence the source of income for the hundreds of hotels, boarding houses, shops, and travel agencies along both shores of the Falls and gorge gave extra reason to keep the peace.

So did the importance of the Welland Canal. The channels of the Erie Canal, and its successor the Barge Canal, were never

When Irish patriots attempted to conquer the Niagara peninsula in June, 1866, this locomotive puffed trainloads of Canada's volunteer soldiers in from Toronto and Saint Catherines to repel the invasion.

dug deep enough to handle big ships. The Welland Canal's twenty-seven-mile channel through Canada remained the only means by which big ships could travel between the upper Great Lakes and the Atlantic. After 1860, the huge production of iron ore, grain, and manufactured goods around the upper Great Lakes and the increase in population there made the Welland Canal one of the busiest and most important waterways in the world.

(68)

The government of Upper Canada (now Ontario) enlarged the Welland Canal in 1871 so that its channel and locks would be large enough for oceangoing ships. But traffic between the St. Lawrence and the upper lakes increased so much between 1871

Horsepower and coal-fueled steam engines provided the power for the enlargement of the Welland Canal during the 1870's.

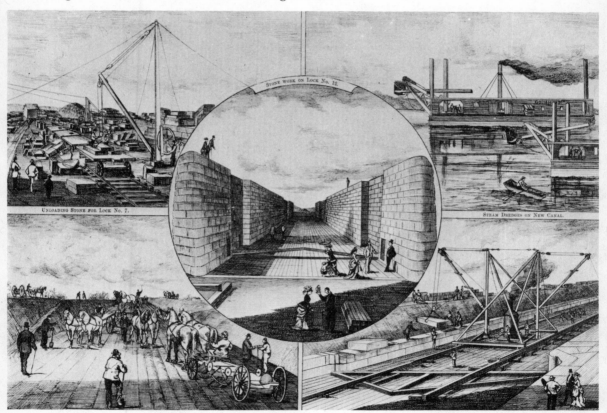

Twin locks on the Welland Canal provide two-way traffic for oceangoing ships climbing around Niagara Falls.

and 1910 that a second program of enlarging the canal had to be started in 1912. This overhaul and enlargement continued for twenty years and cost $130,000,000.

American dependence on the Welland Canal and the growth of good-neighbor practices between the Americans and the Canadians along the shores of the Niagara were strong influences for friendlier relations between the two governments.

Another important reason for becoming good neighbors was found in 1880 when the tumbling waters of the Niagara were first used to make light.

Niagara Power

The English word "electricity" comes from the ancient Greek word for "amber." Thousands of years ago, Greeks learned that a magnetic force could be built up in a piece of amber by rubbing it briskly with a cloth. Finally, about the time Chabert Joncaire built the portage road, experiments began to demonstrate that quantities of this "electricity" could be produced by machine. The first electric arc lights in North America were installed in a Philadelphia department store in 1878. Two years later, Thomas Alva Edison patented the carbon-filament light bulb. Then engineers began the giant task of harnessing the power of Niagara for Niagara Power.

During the spring of 1880, a brush dynamo was attached to a waterwheel in Prospect Park, behind the Falls. It lit two arc lights installed near the park's fountain. Railroads ran excursion trains in from New York City, Cleveland, and Detroit for this "first public viewing of electricity at Niagara Falls." Soon a d.c. generator installed in the canal of a paper mill below the Falls furnished "the light of 2,000 candles."

A canal to provide waterpower for mills down the gorge had been built around the Falls and down the American shore during the 1850's. The first commercial power plant on the Niagara

The vast power produced by the Great Lakes' drainage down the drop of the Niagara "throat" first lured millers there in 1764. Construction of the first hydroelectric generator plant in the gorge in 1893 began the use of Niagara Power in homes and factories eastward to New York City, Boston, and Quebec and westward to the shores of Lake Superior.

was built on this canal in 1895. It was named the Adams Station, and could produce 3730 kilowatts (5,000 horsepower).

The first power stations at the bottom of the gorge below the Falls were built between 1900 and 1910. They produced about 80,000 kilowatts.

(73)

The amount of water being drawn out of the Upper Niagara to operate mills and power plants caused complaints along both shores of the river. Hotelmen and shopkeepers prophesied that "They'll dry up the Falls and ruin all our business."

Statesmen and engineers from the United States and Canada conferred in 1909. They drew up a treaty that limited the use of Niagara water by mills and power plants and so enabled a contant display of "splash and thunder" over the precipice of the Falls.

Transmission lines became more efficient. Niagara Power began to replace steam engines, waterwheels, and oil lamps, east to the Hudson Valley and west to the shore of Lake Huron. The idea grew for the construction of an *artificial* Niagara Falls.

The total drop in elevation of the Niagara River between Lake Erie and Lake Ontario is 326 feet. But only 176 feet of this plunge occurs at the Falls. The upper rapids, above the Falls, are caused by an elevation drop of 70 feet. Another elevation drop of 80 feet occurs in the rapids down the gorge, below the Falls.

A power plant that drew its water from the upper Niagara, near Lake Erie, the engineers planned, could be piped to the top of the gorge. Plunged down the cliff there, it would provide the vast force of a waterfall 300 feet high.

Engineers planned a power plant to be built at the top of the gorge. Water could be piped to it from the upper Niagara, near Lake Erie. As it plunged down the cliff, the water would provide the force of a waterfall 300 feet high.

The same principles were used at the Schoellkopf Plant at the foot of the gorge on the American shore. Its turbines, powered

Sir Adam Beck became mayor of London, Ontario in 1902. He introduced the bill creating the Hydroelectric Power Commission of Ontario and became its first chairman. The huge power plants on the Canadian side of the gorge are named for him.

by a water drop of 215 feet, produced 365,000 kilowatts.

Ontario Hydro built the Sir Adam Beck No. 2 plant during the 1950's. It has a capacity of 1,200,000 kilowatts (1,600,000 horsepower) produced by sixteen units.

Again, there were whispered fears about drying up the Falls. But Canada and the United States had been allies during the two world wars. The suspicions and hatreds of the French and Indian Wars, the American Revolution, the War of 1812, the Patriot War of 1837, the Confederate raiders of 1864, and the Irish Patriot invasion of 1866 were pretty much forgotten.

A Good-Neighbor commission of Americans and Canadians drew up another Niagara Water Treaty. In it, they worked out

The mighty sources of Niagara Power for both Canada and the United States are Canada's Sir Adam Beck Generating Stations 1 and 2 (right) and New York's Robert Moses Power Plant (left).

a method that would provide water for larger Niagara Power plants as well as for the Falls. A flow of at least 100,000 cubic feet of water — 750,000 gallons — per second is permitted to tumble over the Falls during "the daylight hours of the tourist season," April 1 to October 30. But at night and during the winter months the Niagara Power plants can reduce the flow of the Falls to 50,000 cubic feet per second.

A rockslide destroyed most of the Schoellkopf Plant in 1956. The New York Power Authority began construction of a new Niagara Power project during March, 1958, at a cost of $745 million. The final unit went into operation on May 21, 1962.

The project's intake is located on the upper Niagara, two and a half miles behind the Falls. Water flows five miles to a 20-billion-gallon-capacity storage reservoir. From there, water is released through a forebay to thirteen huge pipes — they are called penstocks — that plunge 313 feet down the concrete and steel cliff of the Robert Moses Plant to the generator units on the shore of the lower Niagara. This man-made Niagara can produce 2,190,000 kilowatts. It is the largest hydroelectric development in North America.

The opening of the Robert Moses State Parkway along the route of Joncaire's road completed Niagara's transformation for — and actually by — Niagara Power. The colored lights that rainbow the Falls at night, the elevators of the vista towers on each shore, the aero-cars humming across the gorge near the Great Blondin teeter-route are all symbols of the new Niagara Power — a force so thoroughly harnessed by technology that it simultaneously lights homes as far west as Lake Superior and as

This diorama in the Power Vista on the Robert Moses Parkway shows the network of dynamos, reservoirs, water channels, and switchyards that produce Niagara Power.

far east as Massachusetts, powers the subway trains of New York City and Montreal, and in a thousand other ways enables a better life for 60 million good neighbors in Canada and the United States. The tremendous importance of Niagara Power was dramatically shown on November 9–10, 1965, when a minor failure at the Sir Adam Beck No. 2 plant blacked out parts of Ontario and Quebec and much of the northeastern United States.

The new age of good neighbors was further demonstrated with the construction of the St. Lawrence Seaway between 1954 and 1958. Then the eight locks and the twenty-six-mile channel of the Welland Canal were widened and dredged to a channel depth of twenty-seven feet. United States President Dwight Eisenhower and Queen Elizabeth II of England formally opened the seaway in June, 1959. Since then, cargo ships as big as twenty-five thousand tons gross have been able to make the twenty-three-hundred-mile journey from the mouth of the St. Lawrence to Chicago, Port Arthur, Duluth, and other head-of-the-lakes ports. The cargo lifted over the Niagara Ridge via the Welland Canal and Niagara Power averages 30 million tons a year.

A Niagara Chronology

Approx. 20,000 B.C.   The melt-off of the glacier that covers most of our Northeast and Midwest begins to gouge out the Niagara channel.

20,000 B.C. on   The torrents of water from the melt-off cut the crest of Niagara Falls south toward Lake Erie. This creates the gorge of the lower Niagara and plows out the channels of the St. Lawrence, Mohawk, and Hudson rivers.

A.D. 160   The Moundbuilders, a strong nation of midwestern Indians, operate a trading post and fort atop the gorge, near the site of Lewiston.

November, 1615   Etienne Brulé, a young aide to Samuel de Champlain, becomes (reputedly) the first European explorer to see Niagara Falls.

1641–60   The Five Nations (the Iroquois) conquer the area. They give the waterfall the name "Niagara" meaning the "Throatway."

January, 1679   La Salle builds Fort Conde on the site of Fort Niagara, develops the portage trail, and starts construction of the *Griffon* behind the Falls.

July, 1679   The *Griffon* begins the first sailing-ship cruise of the upper lakes.

August, 1687   The French build Fort Denonville near the ruins of Fort Conde.

September 15, 1688   Fort Denonville abandoned. A Jesuit builds an oak cross, eighteen feet high, as a memorial to the eighty soldiers and officers killed by Indians or "the fevers" during the thirteen-month occupation.

Spring, 1721   Louis Joncaire builds the trading post, *Magazin Royal* at the foot of Crawl-on-All-Fours bluff, behind Lewiston.

June, 1726   Chaussegros de Lery, the engineer-architect responsible for the new forts and city wall of Quebec, designs and begins to build the House of Peace at Fort Niagara.

Summer, 1750   Louis Joncaire's son, Chabert, builds Fort Little Niagara near the site of La Salle's shipyard. Then, as master of the Niagara portage, Chabert develops the portage trail into a wagon road and develops a horse ranch on the River of Horses (Buffalo Creek).

April, 1753   The twenty-three hundred soldiers and Indians of the French Army of the Beautiful River cross the Niagara portage to begin the conquest of the Ohio Valley.

Summer, 1755   The cannon captured at the French-Indian defeat of General Braddock's army near Fort Duquesne (the site of present-day Pittsburgh) are hauled to Fort Niagara and installed on its ramparts.

July, 1759   Brigadier General John Prideaux, with British regulars, colonials, and Indians, begins siege of Fort Niagara. General Prideaux killed on July 21. Sir William Johnson takes command of the expedition.

July 24, 1759   A force of six hundred French and fifteen hundred Indians from the upper lakes make a desperate effort to raise the siege of Fort Niagara. Colonials and Iroquois ambush them in the forest of La Belle Famille, two miles from the fort. The fort surrenders to Sir William Johnson on July 25.

September 14, 1763   Seneca allies of the Pontiac Rebellion ambush a British wagon train at Devil's Hole, near the site of the present-day Robert Moses Niagara Power Plant. They kill and scalp eighty-eight wagonmen and soldiers.

Summer, 1764   Captain John Montresor, chief engineer for the British army in North America, designs and builds an elevator system to carry supplies and trade goods over the Crawl-on-All-Fours bluff. This was the first railroad ever built in North America.

Summer, 1775   Fort Niagara becomes a stronghold for Royalist and Indian refugees of the American Rebellion.

1776–1783   Butler's Rangers, Sir John Johnson's Royal Greens, and Joseph Brant's Mohawks use Fort Niagara as headquarters base for their raids against American settlements on the New York and Pennsylvania frontiers.

Winter, 1779   More than five thousand Indians flee to Niagara after the Clinton-Sullivan expedition conquers the Six Nations homelands and burns the villages and crops. Hundreds starve or freeze to death in huts and caves along the gorge during the winter.

Spring, 1780   Governor William Haldimand orders the development of farms along the Niagara shore. He calls the program the Niagara Plan for Edible Annex. This begins the civilian settlement of Upper Canada.

1791   The province of Upper Canada created by Great Britain. The village of Newark, near the Niagara's mouth, becomes the capital.

Late Summer, 1792   The first session of the parliament of Upper Canada meets in Navy Hall, Newark. The delegates outlaw slavery in the province.

1794   Black slaves from the United States begin their flight across the Niagara to freedom in Canada. During the next seventy years, more than seventy-five thousand slaves dare the perils of the Underground Railway to reach Upper Canada, the Land of Promise.

June 1, 1796   Jay's Treaty between the United States and Great Britain turns the British forts on the eastern shore of the Niagara over to the United States and establishes the international boundary line at the center of the river and falls. Thus, the American settlement begun on the Niagara and the east side of the falls becomes the American Falls.

1808   Settlers choose the name *Buffalo* for their new village on the River of Horses.

June 17, 1812   The United States Congress approves a declaration of war against Great Britain and orders invasions of Upper Canada via Detroit and Niagara.

October 13, 1812   Colonel Winfield Scott and nine hundred American soldiers surrender to the Upper Canadians at Queenston Heights. Sir Isaac Brock, "Victor of Detroit," is killed during the early afternoon of the fourteen-hour battle.

May 27, 1813   American troops capture Forts George and Erie, thus releasing warships for Perry's fleet, trapped at Black Rock.

December 18–30, 1813 Upper Canada troops capture Fort Niagara by the bayonet, then burn the American villages of Lewiston, Black Rock, and Buffalo.

July 25, 1814 The Battle of Lundy's Lane, deadliest of the War of 1812, is fought between sunset and midnight a mile from the Falls on the Upper Canada shore. The United States loses 860 soldiers; the Canadians lose 878.

December 24, 1814 The Treaty of Ghent ends the War of 1812. Known as the Peace of Christmas Eve, it reestablishes the center of the Niagara River as the international boundary line.

April, 1818 The Rush-Bagot Agreement between the United States and Great Britain ends the race to build large navies on the Great Lakes.

Fall, 1824 Upper Canada begins construction of the Welland Canal to enable ships to climb past the Falls between Lakes Erie and Ontario. The canal locks are 110 feet long and 22 feet wide and can handle boats of eight-foot draft or less.

Fall, 1825 Governor DeWitt Clinton and hundreds of New York notables officially open the Erie Canal by sailing from Buffalo to Albany, with parades, cannon salutes, and a Grand Canal ball at each village.

December 29, 1837 Upper Canada soldiers seize the steamship *Caroline* at Schlosser's Landing on the American shore of the upper Niagara, set it afire, and send it over the Falls. This incident of Upper Canada's Patriot War almost starts a third war between the United States and Great Britain.

August, 1860 The Prince of Wales — the future Edward VII of Great Britain — visits Niagara Falls but declines the invitation from the Great Blondin to be carried piggyback across the gorge on a tightrope.

1861 Great Britain's sympathy for the Southern cause during the American Civil War prompts her government to bar all Union vessels from the Welland Canal. The fear of another war with England causes drastic enlargement of the American forts on the Niagara and crisis weeks of martial law in Lewiston, Niagara Falls, Black Rock, and Buffalo.

June 1, 1866 Irish patriots, called the Fenians, invade Upper Canada from Buffalo. They plan to seize the Welland Canal and hold it until Queen Victoria gives Ireland its freedom. The invasion fails. But it hastens the petition to the British Parliament to unite the provinces in North America into the Dominion of Canada.

The 1870's The Niagara becomes "the honeymooners' paradise."

December 14, 1881 The first public demonstration of electricity from the Niagara is held at Black Rock. A d.c. generator supplies "the light of 2,000 candles."

1895 The first large-scale production of Niagara Power begins at the Adams power plant on the upper rapids.

September 6, 1901 President McKinley assassinated at Pan-American Exposition in Buffalo.

October 4, 1901 Mrs. Anna Edson Taylor, a schoolteacher, survives a ride over the Falls and through the whirlpool rapids in a padded barrel.

1962 Completion of the Robert Moses Niagara Power Plant makes possible the production of 13 billion kilowatt hours per year on the American shore of the gorge.

July, 1964   Robert Moses Parkway opened along the approximate route of the French-British portage road.

November 9–10, 1965   A minor defect at Niagara triggers the massive electric-power failure that paralyzes the northeastern United States and large areas of Ontario and Quebec.

June 24, 1967   Soviet Premier Aleksei Kosygin visits Niagara Falls.

Index

Abolitionists, 32
Adams Station, 73, 85
American Revolution, 4, 23-26, 82
Audubon, John James, 51

Barge Canal, 67
Batavia, 37
Black Rock, 31, 42, 43, 48, 83, 84, 85
Blacks, 29-33, 83
Blondin, The Great. *See* Gravelet, Jean
  François
Braddock, General Edward, 20, 81
Brant, Joseph, 23, 29, 82
Brantford, 29
British. *See* Great Britain
Brock, Sir Isaac, 40, 83
Brown, Jacob, 43, 45
Brown, Noah, 48-49
Brulé, Etienne, 80
Buffalo, New York, 23, 31, 37, 44, 46,
  48, 50, 83, 84, 85
Buffalo Creek, 23, 37, 81
  See also Buffalo, New York; River of
    Horses
Burlington Bay, 28
Burlington Heights, 42
Butler, John, 23
Butler's Rangers, 23, 25, 82

Calhoun, John C., 39

Canal era, 46-50
Cave of the Winds, 54, 55
Cayuga Creek, 16, 18
Cayuga Indians, 11, 21, 29
Champlain, Lake, 13
Champlain, Samuel de, 13, 80
Chippawa, 29
  Battle of, 44
Civil War, 64
Clay, Henry, 38
Clemens, Samuel L. (Mark Twain), 54,
  64
Clench, John, 31
Clinton, DeWitt, 46, 84
Clinton, General James, 26
Clinton-Sullivan expedition, 26, 82
Colcord, Harry, 62
Crawl-on-All-Fours Hill, 18, 23, 35, 81,
  82

Daredevils, 58-66
De Lery, Gaspard Chaussegros, 17-18,
  81
Detroit River, 36
Devil's Hole, 22, 54, 82
Drummond, General Gordon, 45
Dutch, 13, 15

Eisenhower, Dwight, 79
Electricity, 72-79, 85

Elizabeth II, 79
Erie Canal, 46-48, 67, 84
Erie, Lake, 4, 7, 8, 18, 23, 29, 32, 42,
    46-48, 74, 80
  Battle of, 42
Erie, Pennsylvania, 41, 42

Farming, 25, 28-29
Fenians, 85
Five Nations, 11, 13, 15-16, 80
Fort Chippawa, 36
Fort Conde, 16, 80
Fort Denonville, 81
Fort Erie, 23, 36, 49, 83
Fort George, 35, 43, 54, 83
Fort Little Niagara, 18, 81
Fort Niagara, 20-25, 27, 35, 37, 43, 46,
    54, 80, 81, 82, 84
Fort Oswego, 37
France. See French
Franklin, Benjamin, 51
French, 4, 13, 15, 20, 21, 34, 81, 82
French and Indian Wars, 4, 20, 21, 81

Genesee River, 37
George III, 29
Goat Island, 52, 66
Goldsmith, Oliver, 51
Graham, Carlisle, 64
Grand River, 29, 30, 31, 41
Grass Island, 65
Gravelet, Jean François (the Great
    Blondin), 58-64, 85
Great Britain, 4, 20, 21-26, 34-36, 38,
    81-85
Great Lakes, 3, 4, 8, 10, 26, 34, 36, 46,
    68, 69, 84
  See also names of individual lakes
Griffon, 16, 80

Haldimand, General Frederick, 25-26,
    82

Henson, Reverend Josiah, 33
Honeycutt, Jim, 66
Horseshoe Fall, 54, 66
House of Peace, 17, 18, 81
Hudson, Henry, 13
Hudson River, 46, 80
Hudson River Valley, 4, 9, 15
Huron Indians, 11, 13, 15
Huron, Lake, 4, 15, 74

Indians, 3, 4, 7, 8-26, 29, 30, 34, 39, 41,
    80-82
  See also names of individual tribes
Iroquois, 15, 16, 80, 82

Jay, John, 34
Jay's Treaty, 34-35, 83
Johnson, Sir William, 21, 23, 81, 82
Joncaire, Chabert, 18, 81
Joncaire, Louis, 17, 18, 81
Judah, Theodore DeHone, 50

Kingston, 28, 36
Kosygin, Aleksei, 86

La Belle Famille, 21, 46, 82
Lafayette, Marquis de, 51
La Salle, Robert Cavelier, Sieur de, 16,
    80
Lewiston, 10, 18, 41, 43, 80, 81, 84, 85
Lincoln, Abraham, 64
Lockport, 48, 50
Loyalists, 23, 25, 26
Lundy's Lane, 44-45, 84

Madison, President James, 39
Magazin Royal, 17, 81
Maid of the Mist, 54, 60, 62, 66
McKinley, William, 85
Michigan, Lake, 4
Mohawk Indians, 11, 13, 29, 82
Mohawk River, 37, 46, 80

Mohawk River Valley, 4, 9
Montreal, 18, 39
Montresor, John, 23, 35, 82
Moundbuilders, 11, 80

Negroes. *See* Blacks; Slavery
Newark (Niagara-on-the-Lake), 27, 29,
    35, 36, 43, 49, 83
New France, 15
New York Power Authority, 77
New York State, 4, 8, 9, 11, 15, 16, 23,
    25, 37, 40, 41, 46
Niagara Falls
    artists and, 53
    daredevils, 58-66, 85
    descriptions of, 51-56
    geology, 4-7, 80
    name, 3
    power, 72-79, 85
    statistics, 3, 74, 77
Niagara-on-the-Lake, *See* Newark
Niagara Plan of Edible Annex, 26, 82
Niagara Power, 3, 4, 72-79, 85
Niagara River, 30, 34, 35, 37, 39, 40,
    43, 74, 80
Niagara Water Treaty, 75

Ohio, 8, 9, 11
Oneida Indians, 21
Onondaga Indians, 11, 37
Ontario, 9, 28
    See also Upper Canada
Ontario hydro, 4, 75
Ontario, Lake, 4, 7, 8, 11, 15, 18, 27,
    28, 32, 36, 37, 74
Oswego River, 37

Patriots' War, 31, 84
Perry, Oliver Hazard, 41-42, 83
Pike, Zebulon, 41, 42
Pontiac, Chief, 21
Pontiac War, 21-23, 82

Port Colborne, 49
Power failure of 1965, 79, 86
Prideaux, John, 21, 81
Puritans, 15
Put-in-Bay, 42

Quebec, 9, 18
Queenston, 29, 39-41, 83

Railroad, 24, 35, 50, 82
Reed, Samuel B., 50
Revolutionary War. *See* American
    Revolution
River of Horses, 18, 23, 37, 81, 83
    See also Buffalo, New York;
        Buffalo Creek
Robert Moses Plant, 77, 85
Rochester, 37
Rome, New York, 37
Royal Rangers. *See* Butler's Rangers
Rush-Bagot Treaty, 45, 67, 84

Sackets Harbor, 41
St. Lawrence River, 3, 4, 27, 69, 80
St. Lawrence River Valley, 11, 13, 15
St. Lawrence Seaway, 3, 79
Schoellkopf Plant, 74, 77
Scott, Winfield, 41, 43-45, 83
Second Mountain, 10
Seneca Indians, 3, 11, 18, 21, 29, 82
Sir Adam Beck No. 1 plant, 74
Sir Adam Beck No. 2 plant, 75, 79
Six Nations, 16, 20, 21, 23, 25, 82
Slavery, 29-33, 83
Stowe, Harriet Beecher, 33
Sullivan, General John, 26
Superior, Lake, 4

Taylor, Annie Edson, 64-66, 85
Toronto, 28, 42
Tourism, 50-57
Trollope, Frances, 51

Tuscorora Indians, 16
Twain, Mark (Samuel L. Clemens), 54, 64

Underground Railroad, 32-33, 83
Upper Canada, 26-36, 69
  first Parliament, 28, 29, 83
  War of 1812, 39-44, 82-85

Wales, Prince of, 62-64, 84
Walk-on-the-Water, 49

War of 1812, 4, 30-31, 39-45, 54, 83-84
Washington, George, 20, 25
Welland Canal, 46, 48, 67, 68, 69, 71, 79, 84, 85
Wells, Fargo & Company, 50
Whirlpool Rapids, 64
Wilde, Oscar, 56
Woodward, Roger and Deanne, 66

York, 28, 42